Francis Frith's
ISLE OF MAN

PHOTOGRAPHIC MEMORIES

Francis Frith's
ISLE OF MAN

◆

Clive Hardy

FRITH
BOOK Co

First published in the United Kingdom in 1999 by
Frith Book Company Ltd

British Library Cataloguing in Publication Data

Isle of Man
Clive Hardy
ISBN 1-85937-065-9

Frith Book Company Ltd
Frith's Barn, Teffont,
Salisbury, Wiltshire SP3 5QP
Tel: +44 (0) 1722 716 376
Email: frithbook.co.uk

Printed and bound in Great Britain

CONTENTS

FRANCIS FRITH: *Victorian Pioneer*

FRANCIS FRITH, Victorian founder of the world-famous photographic archive, was a complex and multitudinous man. A devout Quaker and a highly successful Victorian businessman, he was both philosophic by nature and pioneering in outlook.

By 1855 Francis Frith had already established a wholesale grocery business in Liverpool, and sold it for the astonishing sum of £200,000, which is the equivalent today of over £15,000,000. Now a multi-millionaire, he was able to indulge his passion for travel. As a child he had pored over travel books written by early explorers, and his fancy and imagination had been stirred by family holidays to the sublime mountain regions of Wales and Scotland. 'What a land of spirit-stirring and enriching scenes and places!' he had written. He was to return to these scenes of grandeur in later years to 'recapture the thousands of vivid and tender memories', but with a different purpose. Now in his thirties, and captivated by the new science of photography, Frith set out on a series of pioneering journeys to the Nile regions that occupied him from 1856 until 1860.

INTRIGUE AND ADVENTURE

He took with him on his travels a specially-designed wicker carriage that acted as both dark-room and sleeping chamber. These far-flung journeys were packed with intrigue and adventure. In his life story, written when he was sixty-three, Frith tells of being held captive by bandits, and of fighting 'an awful midnight battle to the very point of surrender with a deadly pack of hungry, wild dogs'. Sporting flowing Arab costume, Frith arrived at Akaba by camel seventy years before Lawrence, where he encountered 'desert princes and rival sheikhs, blazing with jewel-hilted swords'.

During these extraordinary adventures he was assiduously exploring the desert regions bordering the Nile and patiently recording the antiquities and peoples with his camera. He was the first photographer to venture beyond the sixth cataract. Africa was still the mysterious 'Dark Continent', and Stanley and Livingstone's historic meeting was a decade into the future. The conditions for picture taking confound belief. He laboured for hours in his wicker dark-room in the sweltering heat of the desert, while the volatile chemicals fizzed dangerously in their trays. Often he was forced to work in remote tombs and caves where conditions were cooler. Back in London he exhibited his photographs and was 'rapturously cheered' by members of the Royal Society. His reputation as a photographer was made overnight. An eminent modern historian has likened their impact on the population of the time to that on our own generation of the first photographs taken on the surface of the moon.

VENTURE OF A LIFE-TIME

Characteristically, Frith quickly spotted the opportunity to create a new business as a specialist publisher of photographs. He lived in an era of immense and sometimes violent change. For the poor in the early part of Victoria's reign work was a drudge and the hours long, and people had precious little free time to enjoy themselves.

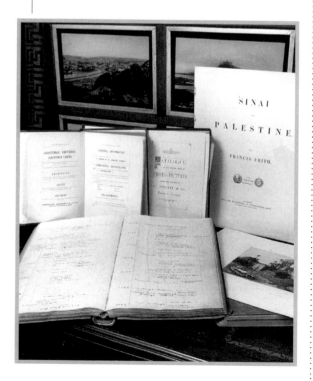

Most had no transport other than a cart or gig at their disposal, and had not travelled far beyond the boundaries of their own town or village. However, by the 1870s, the railways had threaded their way across the country, and Bank Holidays and half-day Saturdays had been made obligatory by Act of Parliament. All of a sudden the ordinary working man and his family were able to enjoy days out and see a little more of the world.

With characteristic business acumen, Francis Frith foresaw that these new tourists would enjoy having souvenirs to commemorate their days out. In 1860 he married Mary Ann Rosling and set out with the intention of photographing every city, town and village in Britain. For the next thirty years he travelled the country by train and by pony and trap, producing fine photographs of seaside resorts and beauty spots that were keenly bought by millions of Victorians. These prints were painstakingly pasted into family albums and pored over during the dark nights of winter, rekindling precious memories of summer excursions.

THE RISE OF FRITH & CO

Frith's studio was soon supplying retail shops all over the country. To meet the demand he gathered about him a small team of photographers, and published the work of independent artist-photographers of the calibre of Roger Fenton and Francis Bedford. In order to gain some understanding of the scale of Frith's business one only has to look at the catalogue issued by Frith & Co in 1886: it runs to some 670

court card, but there was little room for illustration. In 1899, a year after Frith's death, a new card measuring 5.5 x 3.5 inches became the standard format, but it was not until 1902 that the divided back came into being, with address and message on one face and a full-size illustration on the other. *Frith & Co* were in the vanguard of postcard development, and Frith's sons Eustace and Cyril continued their father's monumental task, expanding the number of views offered to the public and recording more and more places in Britain, as the coasts and countryside were opened up to mass travel.

Francis Frith died in 1898 at his villa in Cannes, his great project still growing. The archive he created continued in business for another seventy years. By 1970 it contained over a third of a million pictures of 7,000 cities, towns and villages. The massive photographic record Frith has left to us stands as a living monument to a special and very remarkable man.

pages, listing not only many thousands of views of the British Isles but also many photographs of most European countries, and China, Japan, the USA and Canada – note the sample page shown above from the hand-written *Frith & Co* ledgers detailing pictures taken. By 1890 Frith had created the greatest specialist photographic publishing company in the world, with over 2,000 outlets – more than the combined number that Boots and WH Smith have today! The picture on the right shows the *Frith & Co* display board at Ingleton in the Yorkshire Dales. Beautifully constructed with mahogany frame and gilt inserts, it could display up to a dozen local scenes.

POSTCARD BONANZA

The ever-popular holiday postcard we know today took many years to develop. In 1870 the Post Office issued the first plain cards, with a pre-printed stamp on one face. In 1894 they allowed other publishers' cards to be sent through the mail with an attached adhesive halfpenny stamp. Demand grew rapidly, and in 1895 a new size of postcard was permitted called the

Frith's Archive: *A Unique Legacy*

FRANCIS FRITH'S legacy to us today is of immense significance and value, for the magnificent archive of evocative photographs he created provides a unique record of change in 7,000 cities, towns and villages throughout Britain over a century and more. Frith and his fellow studio photographers revisited locations many times down the years to update their views, compiling for us an enthralling and colourful pageant of British life and character.

We tend to think of Frith's sepia views of Britain as nostalgic, for most of us use them to conjure up memories of places in our own lives with which we have family associations. It often makes us forget that to Francis Frith they were records of daily life as it was actually being lived in the cities, towns and villages of his day. The Victorian age was one of great and often bewildering change for ordinary people, and though the pictures evoke an impression of slower times, life was as busy and hectic as it is today.

We are fortunate that Frith was a photographer of the people, dedicated to recording the minutiae of everyday life. For it is this sheer wealth of visual data, the painstaking chronicle of changes in dress, transport, street layouts, buildings, housing, engineering and landscape that captivates us so much today. His remarkable images offer us a powerful link with the past and with the lives of our ancestors.

TODAY'S TECHNOLOGY

Computers have now made it possible for Frith's many thousands of images to be accessed almost instantly. In the Frith archive today, each photograph is carefully 'digitised' then stored on a CD Rom. Frith archivists can locate a single photograph amongst thousands within seconds. Views can be catalogued and sorted under a variety of categories of place and content to the immediate benefit of researchers. Inexpensive reference prints can be created for them at the touch of a mouse button, and a wide range of books and other printed materials assembled and published for a wider, more general readership - in the next twelve months over a hundred Frith local history titles will be published! The

See Frith at www. francisfrith.co.uk

day-to-day workings of the archive are very different from how they were in Francis Frith's time: imagine the herculean task of sorting through eleven tons of glass negatives as Frith had to do to locate a particular sequence of pictures! Yet the archive still prides itself on maintaining the same high standards of excellence laid down by Francis Frith, including the painstaking cataloguing and indexing of every view.

It is curious to reflect on how the internet now allows researchers in America and elsewhere greater instant access to the archive than Frith himself ever enjoyed. Many thousands of individual views can be called up on screen within seconds on one of the Frith internet sites, enabling people living continents away to revisit the streets of their ancestral home town, or view places in Britain where they have enjoyed holidays. Many overseas researchers welcome the chance to view special theme selections, such as transport, sports, costume and ancient monuments.

We are certain that Francis Frith would have heartily approved of these modern developments, for he himself was always working at the very limits of Victorian photographic technology.

THE VALUE OF THE ARCHIVE TODAY

Because of the benefits brought by the computer, Frith's images are increasingly studied by social historians, by researchers into genealogy and ancestory, by architects, town planners, and by teachers and schoolchildren involved in local history projects. In addition, the archive offers every one of us a unique opportunity to examine the places where we and our families have lived and worked down the years. Immensely successful in Frith's own era, the archive is now, a century and more on, entering a new phase of popularity.

THE PAST IN TUNE WITH THE FUTURE

Historians consider the Francis Frith Collection to be of prime national importance. It is the only archive of its kind remaining in private ownership and has been valued at a million pounds. However, this figure is now rapidly increasing as digital technology enables more and more people around the world to enjoy its benefits.

Francis Frith's archive is now housed in an historic timber barn in the beautiful village of Teffont in Wiltshire. Its founder would not recognize the archive office as it is today. In place of the many thousands of dusty boxes containing glass plate negatives and an all-pervading odour of photographic chemicals, there are now ranks of computer screens. He would be amazed to watch his images travelling round the world at unimaginable speeds through network and internet lines.

The archive's future is both bright and exciting. Francis Frith, with his unshakeable belief in making photographs available to the greatest number of people, would undoubtedly approve of what is being done today with his lifetime's work. His photographs, depicting our shared past, are now bringing pleasure and enlightenment to millions around the world a century and more after his death.

THE ISLE OF MAN – *An Introduction*

MUCH OF THE ISLAND'S EARLY history is entwined with that of the Western Isles and the Vikings. In 1066 Harald Hardrada, King of Norway, launched his ill-fated invasion of England and met his death at Stamford Bridge. One of Harald's allies was a chieftain named Godred Crovan, who following the defeat is said to have sought refuge on Man prior to moving to Islay in the Western Isles. After two abortive attempts, Crovan succeeded in mounting a successful invasion of Man in 1079 and reigned there for another sixteen years. It was Crovan who created the Keys, which then consisted of 32 members, sixteen each from Man and the Western Isles. After 1156 only Lewis and Skye continued to send members, four from each island. Following the sale of the Western Isles to Scotland in 1266 only the sixteen Manx members remained, so a further eight members were elected to bring the total back up to twenty-four.

Following Crovan's death the island was plunged into a bloody civil war as two rival chieftains, Ottar and Macmarus, fought each other for supremacy. In a battle at a place called Santwat (which tradition places near Peel), both chieftains were killed, and the island fell into the hands of Magnus Barefoot who arrived in 1098 with 160 longships. Magnus himself was killed in Ireland in 1103; there followed yet more years of confusion until Crovan's youngest son Olaf gained the throne around 1113.

Brought up at the court of Henry I, Olaf reigned for about forty years, during which time the great Cistercian monastery at Rushen Abbey was founded. When Olaf was murdered in 1153 his son Godred was in Norway. Godred's first campaign as King of the Western Isles was to launch an attack against Dublin, but the expedition ended in turmoil when a number of chiefs led by his brother-in-law Somerled, ruler of Argyll, rose in rebellion. In 1156 Godred was defeated in a sea battle off Colonsay and forced to cede territory to Somerled. Two years later Somerled invaded Man and drove out Godred. In 1164 Somerled was killed whilst campaigning against the Scots, and with Norwegian assistance Godred regained Man. He reigned until his death in 1187; the following year his body was taken to Iona for burial.

Norse rule continued until 1265 when King Magnus declared his allegiance to Alexander III of Scotland. The Scots ruled Man for less than a hundred years, for in 1333 it was taken by Edward III. In 1399 the unpopular Richard II was campaigning in Ireland when his cousin Henry took advantage of the situation and seized the throne for himself, reigning as Henry IV. It would be a reign

Stanley Lord of Man on condition that he would present Henry with two falcons on Coronation Day. In order to secure his lines of communication, Stanley was authorised by Henry to fortify the Tower of Liverpool.

At Liverpool the Earls of Derby were treated like princes. On one occasion the weather was so bad that the fourth Earl was forced to wait two weeks in the Tower of Liverpool before he

marked by wars against Scotland and the Welsh, and open rebellion from the barons, notably the Percy family. At Shrewsbury on 21st July 1403 Henry IV fought a combined English and Scottish army led by Henry Percy. Taking part in the battle on the king's side were Sir Hugh and Sir John Stanley. Sir John was lord lieutenant of Ireland, and it was he who secured the Isle of Man for Henry in 1405. Subsequently Henry IV appointed

could embark for Man. It that time he was entertained to banquets, firework displays and morris dancing; it is also said that he attended church wearing a purple cloak. The Earl's household at the Tower was around 140; it included eight gentlemen waiters, eight grooms of the bedchamber, a chaplain and gentlemen ushers. There were also brewers, bakers, a slaughterman, stablehands and so on.

The Stanley family would rule the Man until 1736. Following the death of James II, tenth Earl of Derby, the Lordship of Man passed to his distant relative James Murray, second Duke of Atholl. James Murray took his responsibilities to heart; it was he who granted a series of reforms that culminated in 1737 with what in effect was a Bill of Rights - the right to trail by jury. In 1765 the Revestment Act led to King George III becoming the first regal Lord of Man. The Atholls were compensated for their losses. The third Duke received £70,000 plus an annuity of £2000, and in 1828 the fourth Duke received a further £417,000.

THE ISLE OF MAN AND THE ENGLISH CIVIL WAR

James Stanley, seventh Earl of Derby, became one of the most popular Lords of Man, earning the title 'Y Stanlagh Moar' - The Great Stanley. It was he who changed the island's land laws. At the beginning of Stanley rule, all land was considered to belong to the king and there were no rights of inheritance. James changed the system: all lands were to be leased for periods of three lives, or 21 years, giving tenants and land-owners some measure of security.

Derby was a devout Royalist; when in 1651 Charles II invaded England from Scotland with an army of 8000 foot and 2000 horse, he obeyed his sovereign's wish that he should join up with him in Lancashire. With Sir Thomas Tyldesley, he sailed from the island on 17 August and landed at the mouth of the Wyre, where Fleetwood is now situated, with a force of about three hundred troops. Parliamentarian warships were sent to block-

ade the Wyre and cut off Derby's escape route, but the Earl had already left the area and was marching through Catholic Lancashire attempting to raise the county. The response was not great.

Derby reached Wigan where his force was routed, and Sir Thomas Tyldesley killed, by Parliamentarian troops commanded by Robert Lilurne. Derby, though wounded, escaped. He was cared for by Richard Penderel at Boscobel manor before making his way to Worcester, where he joined the king on 31st August. Though the city was well fortified, Charles was betrayed by his cavalry commander Alexander Leslie, who with his men remained inactive throughout the battle. Forced to flee, the king, accompanied by the Duke of Buckingham, Lord Wilmot, the Earl of Derby and about sixty others escaped to Stourbridge. Derby suggested that the king might find shelter with the Penderel family, and he was taken there.

It was at Boscobel that the king put on his disguise, still intent on walking to London 'in a country fellow's habit'. Derby advised him to rub soot on his face and hands and Lord Wilmot cut off his hair. The King was left in the safe hands of the Penderels and Derby and Wilmot made their own escapes. On the day that Charles and Lord Wilmot arrived at Fecamp in France, they learned that Earl of Derby had been captured and sentenced to death for treason. He was beheaded at Bolton.

INDUSTRY AND TOURISM

Fishing has always been a dangerous occupation. Customs officer David Robinson made a number of visits to Man in the 1780s and 90s, and in 1794 his book 'A Tour Through The Isle of Man' was published. David relates how in 1786 Douglas lighthouse had been all but destroyed in a storm, and all that there was to replace it was a small lantern fixed to a post. In September 1787 David was once again in Douglas. It was the height of the herring season and he estimated that around 400 boats were working the grounds off Clayhead and Laxey. When the fleet had set out the weather had been perfect, but without warning a gale developed forcing the fishermen to head back to Douglas. By the time the first boats were approaching the harbour, high winds and waves were making boat handling difficult. According to David one of the first boats into the harbour somehow managed to dislodge the light, leaving the following craft blind. All hell broke loose. Boats were smashed against rocks and by daybreak the beach was littered with wreckage and bodies.

To encourage exports the British Government offered a bounty of 1s a barrel on herrings destined for the British market, and 2s 6d overseas. The trade was always sensitive to prices. At the beginning of the season, cured white herring would fetch around 3s per hundred - but once the market had been flooded, curers would be lucky to get 1s 6d per hundred. A barrel held about 600 herring; the total cost to the curer was about 12s, and the price at Liverpool docks ranged between £1. 1s and £1. 5s. The art of curing red herring was introduced from Yarmouth in 1771.

A large proportion of the Manx herring catch was sent to Liverpool where it was cured and then shipped to the West Indies as food for slaves. When abolition came in 1834, demand for Manx herrings went into a sharp decline. During the second half of the 19th century it became common practice for boats to go into south-east Irish waters and fish for mackerel from March to June, return to Man for the herring season, and then from October follow the herring into Scottish waters.

The Mischief Act of 1765 attempted to put paid to at least one Manx pastime, smuggling. At least fifty officers and two or three revenue cutters were deployed accordingly. Any inroads they made were soon lost, as smuggling was rife again after 1767 following an Act passed in London setting higher duty levels than those announced by Tynwald. The Act allowed for the import of limited amounts of tea, spirits and tobacco from England, but with smugglers operating to and from the Wirral and remote landing places in Lancashire and Scotland, the Manx received all the tea, spirits and tobacco it could handle. No tea or spirits duties were paid to the English for years.

The Manx proved adept at giving the English Government a run for its duty. Around 1823, some bright spark hit on the idea of using the Manx privilege of importing foreign corn duty-free. Corn was bought from bonded warehouses in Liverpool, and no duty was paid. Shipped over to Man, it was ground into flour and then re-exported to England as Manx flour. This scheme worked for six or seven years before customs and excise rumbled it, by which time the shipments totalled about 25,000 quarters a year. Another venture for a little duty-free involved the importation of machinery into the island on false documentation, claiming that it was for use on Man. The machinery was then exported to customers throughout Europe.

The history of mining on Man, like almost anywhere else, is a tale of boom and bust. Over the years mining operations have been carried out at various locations with varying degrees of success. Foxdale was mined for silver and lead; Laxey for lead, silver and some copper; Ballasherlogue, Ballacorkish and Bradda Head for lead and silver; Maughold Head for haematite, and Langness for copper.

One of the earliest references to mining is a license granted by Edward I to John Comyn, Earl of Buchan, to dig for lead on the Calf of Man. Edward was desperate for lead; he needed it for the string of castles he was building to subjugate Wales. In 1708 John Murray held leases from the Lord of Man on all Manx lead and copper mines on a royalty payment of £3 a tonne. Murray seems to have mined around thirty to forty tonnes a year, but by 1715 he had given up his leases and from then on mining appears to have been carried out on an ad hoc basis.

In 1823 both Laxey and Foxdale were reopened, and the haematite mine at Maughold in 1837. The 1830s and 40s were prosperous years for the Manx mining industry, and from 1870 to the 1880s lead and silver production remained at record levels. During these latter years the industry as a whole was employing over 1000 people, and the Laxey mine was shipping ore worth around £90,000 a year.

Cotton spinning was introduced on Man in 1779 when a mill was opened at Ballasalla, and all went well until 1791 when customs officials at Liverpool realised that it was operating in violation of an Act of 1765 which prohibited the importation of foreign goods, except for flax and hemp, into Britain via

Man. The mill was forced to close, though by 1798 cotton yarns or cotton cloth from Man were being landed at mainland ports free of duty.

There was also a limited amount of ship-building on the island. The Bath Yard at Douglas was capable of building vessels up to 500 cwt, and the steamer King Orry was built there in 1841. Small yards were opened at Ramsey (1834) and Peel (1835), turning out fishing boats and schooners.

During the 19th century tourism grew to such an extent that it dominated the island's economy. In the 1830s, around 25,000 tourists a year braved the unpredictable Irish Sea to visit the island, making the crossing in the ships of the Isle of Man Steam Packet Co and the St George Steam Packet Co. By the 1860s the figure had risen to about 60,000 a year and was still climbing; the 100,000 barrier was broken in the early 1870s. By the beginning of the 20th century well over 400,000 visitors a year came to the island, and a new record was set during the 1913 summer season when the total reached 600,000.

In 1906 visitors could travel to the island from a number of ports. From Liverpool there were two sailings a day with additional services on Fridays and Saturdays. The fares were 3s 6d, or 6s single, 10s 6d return, and the same fare was charged to both Douglas and Ramsey. Other ports offering services were Fleetwood, Heysham, Barrow, Glasgow via Ardrossan, and Silloth via Whitehaven. The sailings from Silloth were twice weekly during the summer season; the Whitehaven route was one sailing per fortnight, but during July and August it was increased to three times weekly. In addition there were regular steam-er services to Belfast and Dublin.

The 1948 season produced a record 625,000 visitors; it seemed as if the tourist industry had simply picked up the ball from where it had been dropped at the start of the Second World War. Tourism continued to be the mainstay of the economy for a number of years, but by the mid-1950s the decline was noticeable. The real slump came in the 1960s as people's expectations changed. Package holidays, the popularity of holidays abroad, and the massive growth in private car owner-ship all influenced people's choice of holiday. By the mid-1980s the number of visitors to the island was about the same as it had been in the 1880s, and the provision of financial serv-ices had become the island's principal source of income.

THE TRANSPORT REVOLUTION

Improved communications both to and from Man, and within Man itself, played a vital role in the economic growth of the island. Prior to 1767 there were few scheduled shipping serv-ices between Man and the mainland, apart from a monthly freight run operated by two sixty-tonne sloops. However, following the transfer of the island's sovereignty to the Crown of England, communications were improved with the introduction of a weekly mail packet service between Douglas and Whitehaven. Trade expanded, and by the early 19th century scheduled freight and packet services linked the island with a num-ber of west coast ports.

Regular steamship services between Douglas and Liverpool were begun in 1822 by the St George Steam Packet Co, and through-out the summer service was adequate. Winter sailings appear to have been sporadic. West coast steamship companies may have been either unable or unwilling to provide the level of year-round services that Man required, a direct result of which was the formation of the Manx-owned Mona's Isle Company in December 1829. The StGSPC retaliated by starting a price war, and soon both companies were slashing fares; the lowest ever advertised by the StGSPC was just 6d each way. The StGSPC also transferred their fast steamer St George from their Irish route to the Isle of Man run in the hope of speeding up the crossing time between Douglas and Liverpool, but unfortunately she was wrecked on Conister Rock a few weeks later, having lost her lost her cable while attempting to ride out a storm. In July 1831 the StGSPC threw in the towel and abandoned all services to Man.

In 1832 the Mona's Isle Co changed its name to the Isle of Man United Steam Packet Co, and bought a second vessel. Three years later the company changed its name once more by dropping the 'United' from its title. Over the next hundred and fifty years the IOMSPCo would not only play a major role in the development of the island, but its ships would serve with distinction in two world wars. By 1880 Manx shipping comprised 185 sailing vessels totalling 9344 grt, and nine steamers totalling 2816 grt; by 1895 the fleet stood at 103 sailing vessels of 7953 grt and 22 steamers of 4897 grt. Another Manx shipping company, the Ramsey Steamship Co, was founded in 1914 to take advantage of a niche in the market for coastal traffic using the smaller Manx and other Irish Sea ports.

The Isle of Man Railway Company was reg-istered in 1870, the aim being to provide rail links between the island's principal towns and Douglas. The line between Douglas and Peel opened for traffic on 2 July 1873, and was followed by the Douglas to Port Erin line on 1 August 1874. The railway adopted the 3 ft gauge used extensively in Ireland, which was cheaper to construct per track mile than the standard gauge used on the mainland. Traffic returns for 1878 included 526,546 passengers and 23,374 tons of freight carried, giving net receipts of £10,454. Even so, the company was strapped for cash, and the proposed line from St John's to Ramsey looked doubtful. In 1877 a new company, the Manx Northern Railway, had stepped into the breach, their line opening for traffic in September 1879. The MNR also leased the Foxdale Railway (which had been promoted in 1882 by Charles Forman, a civil engineer) primarily to provide rail access for the mines at Foxdale, though a passenger service was later added. Having signed a fifty year lease, the MNR were expecting a good return - but the Foxdale line never lived up to expectations. Cheaper ores were becoming available from overseas, and in April 1911 the mining company went into liquidation. The Foxdale Railway was such a drain on the resources of the MNR that by the beginning of the 20th century it was in serious financial trouble. In 1904 the Isle of Man Railway Co absorbed both the MNR and the Foxdale Railway.

On 7 September 1893, services began on a two-and-a-half-mile single-track electric light railway linking Derby Castle with Groudle Glen. The line was based on the American-type interurban, using single-deck bogie cars running on a reserved track. Within a short time the Douglas & Laxey Coast Electric Tramway was formed, the intention being to take control of the line and to finance the building of a double-track extension to Laxey. Construction was soon under way, and the original Douglas to Groudle Glen section was also double-tracked, services commencing throughout on 28 July 1894. Work then began on a further extension from Laxey to Ramsey, but rugged terrain and heavy civil engineering led to slow going and a strain on the company's financial resources. However, the new extension opened as far as Ballure in August 1898 and to Ramsey in July 1899.

DOUGLAS, PORT SKILLION 1895 36730
Douglas Head Lighthouse was erected in 1892,
replacing the sixty year old Red Pier light. In 1786
Douglas harbour lighthouse had been destroyed
during a storm and not rebuilt. The following year
disaster struck the local herring fleet when the
temporary light was somehow dislodged during a
storm, leaving many of the boats blind. The
following morning the beach and rocks were
littered with wreckage and bodies.

DOUGLAS, DOUGLAS HEAD 1907 59154
Douglas Head was always a popular place to
while away a few hours. In 1887 a camera
obscura was opened, and in 1891 the
impressive castellated Marine Drive Gateway
was built. In 1895 the Douglas Southern
Electric Tramway was incorporated to
construct a tramway along the Marine Drive to
Port Soderick.

DOUGLAS, DOUGLAS HEAD 1893 33003

Port Skillion at the foot of Douglas Head was reached by ferry from the harbour, fare 1d, and was used by gentlemen only for open-air bathing. Ladies wishing to avail themselves of the efficacious pleasures to be experienced from sea-bathing were expected to engage the use of a bathing machine.

DOUGLAS, FROM DOUGLAS HEAD 1907 59152

Between May and September 1887, steamers brought nearly 348,000 visitors to the island, though the IOMSPCo. was forced to slash its fares to beat off competition from two new shipping companies who were trying to muscle in on the ever growing Manx holiday traffic. During the 1900 season over 400,000 visitors landed at Douglas.

DOUGLAS, VICTORIA PIER 1907 59160a
When the Victoria Pier was completed in 1872 it gave Douglas the facility to handle steamers regardless of the state of the tide. To increase handling capacity the pier was extended in 1888 to a length of 1620 ft. The two small ferries berthed alongside the pier are the 'Rose' and the 'Thistle', which were used on the Douglas Head service. In 1896 the Liverpool & North Wales Steamship Co introduced a summer service from Llandudno.

DOUGLAS, PROMENADE 1897 39883
A busy scene at the Clock Tower, which was also the terminus of the Douglas Cable Tramway. Cross-bench car No 74 displays the route on its valance: Victoria Street, Woodbourne Road, Ballaquayle Road and Broadway. The line opened in August 1896 and it survived until August 1929. There were proposals to convert the system to overhead electric traction, but these were never carried through.

DOUGLAS, THE CLOCK TOWER & PROMENADE 1897 39885

The Jubilee Clock at the junction of Victoria Street and Loch Promenade was presented to the people of Douglas by George Dumbell in 1887. Dumbell was a banker, a director of the Laxey mines and a Deemster (justice of the Tynwald), but the failure of his bank on Saturday 3rd February 1900 ('Black Saturday') was one of the greatest financial disasters to hit the island.

DOUGLAS, A ROUGH SEA 1903 50661

The Irish Sea can be as flat as a mill pond, but when an easterly, south-easterly or north-easterly gale blows up, this is what happens at Douglas. Sir William Hillary, founder of the RNLI, settled in Douglas in 1808. He became so concerned by the loss of seamen in local wrecks that he erected the Tower of Refuge in Douglas Bay.

DOUGLAS, THE CENTRAL PROMENADE 1896 38769

The tide is well and truly out in this picture, taken as the shadows lengthen on a summer evening in 1896. Had this picture been taken just a few years earlier it would have featured the Douglas Iron Pier, erected opposite the Central Hotel in 1869; it was dismantled in 1892. Note the white areas on the beach - these are piles of linen from nearby hotels being aired and dried.

DOUGLAS, HARRIS PROMENADE 1907 59168

Here we see the hustle and bustle of Douglas in high season. The white castle-like structure in the background is the Falcon Cliff Hotel. During the Second World War it was converted to use as a hospital serving the internment camps established at Douglas.

DOUGLAS, THE SANDS 1907 59166
This photograph shows the Edwardians at play.
These days we take for granted the wearing of
casual or leisure clothing when on holiday, but
in 1907 there was virtually no such thing in
Britain. Many of the people in this picture will
be wearing their Sunday best clothes; the men
might have a few spare collars, pairs of socks
and a spare pair of longjohns; the ladies a
change of underwear and perhaps a couple
of blouses.

DOUGLAS, THE CENTRAL PROMENADE 1896 38770

Prior to the late-Victorian development on this part of the seafront, it would have been possible to see Castle Mona, the residence built in 1804 for Governor James Murray (later Fourth Duke of Atholl) at a cost of £30,000. The residence was converted into a hotel in 1832.

DOUGLAS, THE PROMENADE FROM DERBY CASTLE 1894 34632

The Falcon Cliff Hotel is little more than a dot on the landscape on the left of the picture. Below that, however, is the imposing bulk of the Palace and New Opera House which opened in 1889 and featured what was then the largest ballroom in Europe.

DOUGLAS, DERBY CASTLE AND BAY HOTEL 1894 34634
Built as a private residence in 1834, Derby Castle was converted into an entertainment centre in 1877, featuring variety shows, afternoon concerts and dancing in the ballroom. The site was redeveloped in the early 1970s: the Castle was demolished and replaced by the Summerland complex

DOUGLAS, NEW TRAMWAY STATION 1896 38771a
The Derby Castle terminus of the horse-tramway and the Douglas & Laxey Coast Electric Tramway. When it opened in September 1893, the electric tramway was a modest affair, just a single line running between Douglas and Groudle Glen. The D&LCET was a more ambitious scheme, double track throughout between Douglas and Laxey. In 1896 the fare to Laxey was 1s single, 2s return; Snaefell was 3s 6d return.

DOUGLAS, DERBY CASTLE 1896 37197a

DOUGLAS
Derby Castle 1896

This picture was taken just two years after the horse-trams had been taken over by the operators of the coastal electric tramway. There was talk of converting the horse tramway to electric traction, but nothing ever came of it. In the picture is a double-deck horse-tram; the last of these were phased out in 1949, though old No 14 survived long enough to be shipped off to Clapham Museum in March 1955.

◆

FLEETWOOD
The Isle of Man Packet 1904

The IOMSPCo's 'Mona's Queen' eases out of Fleetwood on a summer sailing. The crossing to the Isle of Man took about three hours; the daily sailing was scheduled to leave after the arrival of the 2.15pm train. There was also a twice-weekly sailing from Fleetwood to Ramsey via Douglas.

FLEETWOOD, MONA'S QUEEN 1904 52171

FLEETWOOD, VIKING 1908 59939

The turbine steamer 'Viking' departing for Douglas. When this picture was taken, the turbine steamers were usually assigned to the Liverpool-Douglas and Heysham-Douglas services.

BELFAST, THE DOUGLAS BOAT 1897 40232

Passengers take an opportunity to experience the sights and sounds of Belfast harbour as the Douglas packet makes her way slowly along. On 3 December 1909 the packet 'Ellan Vannin' was lost with all hands and passengers when she foundered off the entrance to the Mersey, the worst loss in the history of the IOMSPCo.

KIRK BRADDEN, THE OLD CHURCH 1907 59172

One of the famous open-air services which proved so popular with holidaymakers is in full swing at old Kirk Bradden, the mother church of Douglas. The church remains much as it was in the 18th century, with box pews and a three-decker pulpit. The tower was erected in 1773. The obelisk commemorates Lord

Henry Murray.

KIRK BRADDEN, THE OLD CHURCH 1893 33018

As well as the old church, Bradden has a newer one built out of local stone in 1869 (at a cost of £4300) to a design by John Loughborough Pearson. A tower and spire were added in the 1880s, though the spire was eventually removed after suffering storm damage. Both before and between the two world wars the Sunday open-air services at Bradden were so popular that the railway used to lay on special trains.

ST JOHN'S, TYNWALD HILL 1903 50668

Around AD 870 Tynwald Hill was selected by the Vikings as a suitable location, or 'vollr', to hold their open-air assembly, the 'Thing', held annually on old Midsummer's Day. Here freemen settled disputes, and laws for the forthcoming year were announced. Tynwald is a derivation of Thingvollr.

ST JOHN'S, TYNWALD HILL 1903 50669
Tynwald is the oldest unbroken parliament in the world. Godred Crovan created the 'House of Keys', and in his day it included representatives from the Hebrides, but since 1266 it has been comprised solely of Manxmen. The modern Court of Tynwald includes the island's Governor, the ten-member Legislative Council, and the House of Keys.

ST JOHN'S DALE 1893 32894
Late Victorian guidebooks often described the central part of the island in terms such as 'mountainous and beautifully diversified; streams, flowing through narrow leafy glens, with precipitous sides, form numberless cascades. The hilly region ends with the valley of the Sulby, to the north of which is a plain'.

ST JOHN'S, TYNWALD HILL 1903 50669

ST JOHN'S DALE 1893 32894

GLEN HELEN, THE HOTEL 1893 33054
Glen Helen is situated about two miles north of St John's, and was developed from 1850 onwards by a Mr Marsden who named the glen after his daughter.

GLEN HELEN, THE SWISS CHALET 1893 33055
By the 1890s Glen Helen was one of the island's favourite beauty spots, offering visitors extensive facilities. An excellent dinner could be had at the Swiss Cottage Hotel for just 1s 6d. Here, despite the lack of an audience, the band plays on.

GLEN HELEN
The Waterfall 1893

Waterfalls are a feature of Manx glens, and the Rhenass Falls at Glen Helen are probably the finest. Alas, the upper bridge and pathways no longer exist.

GLEN MAYE 1895

Situated to the south of Peel on what is now the A27 road to Colby via Round Table, Glen Maye opens to the sea. It is a great place for those who like to scramble over rocks and paddle in pools. Those who prefer to sit and wait can do so at Ellison's Refreshment Rooms.

GLEN HELEN, THE WATERFALL 1893 33057

GLEN MAYE 1895 36755

GLEN MAYE
In The Glen 1895

Some of the water off the surrounding high ground runs through Glen Rushen and Glen Mooar before entering the sea by way of Glen Maye. The admission price to Glen Maye was cheaper than that to nearby Glen Helen.

PEEL
The Castle and Harbour Entrance 1903

At the height of the season, Peel harbour was often full of fishing boats - Manx, Cornish, Irish and Scottish - as they followed the migrating herring into Scottish waters. In 1881 the Peel herring fleet consisted of 309 boats employing 2163 men and boys; the annual catch was worth around £11,000. By 1891 the local fleet was down to 174 boats employing 860 men and boys with an annual catch valued at just under £3000.

GLEN MAYE, IN THE GLEN 1895   36756

PEEL, THE CASTLE AND HARBOUR ENTRANCE 1903   50647

PEEL, THE TOWN AND THE CASTLE 1893 33045
Magnus Barefoot built a timber fort on St Patrick's Isle between c1098-1103. The bulk of the surviving
fortifications date from the time of Thomas, First Earl of Derby, and were constructed between 1460-1504 as a
defence against Scottish raiders. The tower in the centre of the picture overlooks the causeway linking the islet
with the town, and was probably built by Sir William le Scrope in the 1390s.

PEEL CASTLE, THE ROUND TOWER 1893 33052
Built in the Irish style, the round tower dates from the 10th or 11th centuries and would have been used by the
monks as a place of refuge during raids by pirates or Vikings. It is built from local red sandstone and stands 50 ft
high. Originally it would have had a conical stone roof, but this was replaced by the crenellated top many
centuries ago.

PEEL, ST GERMAN'S CATHEDRAL 1893 *33050*

PEEL, ST GERMAN'S CATHEDRAL 1893 *33051*

PEEL
St German's Cathedral 1893
St German's was begun by Bishop Symon of Argyll in c1230 as the cathedral church of the Sudreys, built on the site of the old parish church of Kirk German. Symon built the chancel, tower and transepts, and his successor Bishop Richard added the nave. The central tower is 68 ft high and has a bell turret rising above it.

PEEL
St German's Cathedral 1893
The crypt of St German's used to house the bishop's prison, where those found guilty by the ecclesiastical court were imprisoned. The bishop's prison was last used in 1780. Inmates were usually those found guilty of adultery, fornication, cursing, or for being drunk and disorderly. The power of the court was undermined in the 1720s when the Governor allowed those sentenced by the church to appeal to a civil court.

PEEL, THE CASTLE 1893 33044

19th-century visitors wishing to get a good view of the town and castle were advised to climb the tower, known as Corrin's folly, on Corrin's Hill (485 ft). It was built by a wealthy nonconformist eccentric to the memory of his wife and family, who were buried nearby. Mr Corrin also wanted to be buried on the hill, but he finished up in the local churchyard. However, he had arranged with some of his friends that if this happened they were to dig him up and bury him near his family. This they did.

PEEL, THE TOWN AND BAY 1895 36758

In the centre foreground of the picture stands St Peter's church, intact at this time, built out of locally quarried Triassic red sandstone and identified by its unusual helm-roof tower. Following a disastrous fire in 1950, only the tower and west window now survive. Also in the picture is the original railway station, the main building of which was replaced in the early years of the 20th century by one designed by Armitage Rigby.

GLEN WYLLIN, THE VILLAGE 1895 36750
The Glen Wyllin area suffers from coastal erosion. In 1951 the old mill stood six metres from the sea, but by 1975 it was on the edge of the cliff. A concrete wall, built to offer protection, is itself now 20 or so metres offshore.

GLEN WYLLIN, THE VIADUCT 1895 36749

BALLAUGH, THE OLD CHURCH 1895 36754

GLEN WYLLIN
The Viaduct 1895

This was one of two viaducts on the Manx Northern line between St John's and Ramsey. The other was at Glen Mooar. Glen Wyllin was only a few minutes walk from Kirkmichael station, and in summer special excursions were run to it from Douglas and Ramsey. The glen was purchased by the IOMR in the 1930s, who added a boating lake, bowling greens and children's play area

◆

BALLAUGH
The Old Church 1895

The oldest church register now extant is that of Ballaugh, and was begun in 1598. The church was one of a number repaired by Thomas Wilson, Bishop of Sodor and Man. In 1717 he had the main body of the building extended by 21 ft.

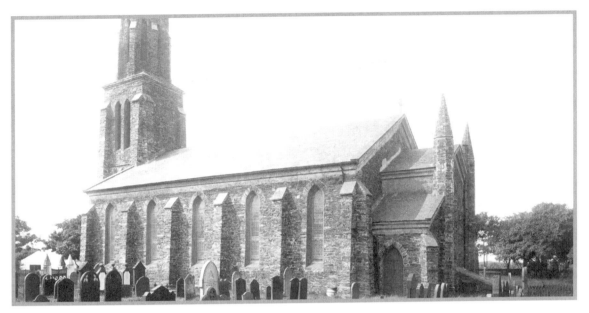

BALLAUGH, THE NEW CHURCH 1895 36753

Designed by John Welch and built in the 1830s, the new Ballaugh church was one of a number built or rebuilt in the early decades of the 19th century. Others include St Patrick's, Jurby (rebuilt 1813); Kirk Michael (rebuilt 1835); St Paul's, Ramsey (erected in 1822); and St Bridget's Roman Catholic Church, Douglas (opened in 1814, the first modern Catholic place of worship to be built on Man).

BALLAUGH, THE VILLAGE 1895 36752

Ballaugh is in the Sheading of Michael. The precise meaning of the word is unclear, but one possibility is that it is derived from 'skeid-thing', a Norse word for a local assembly of the freemen, who, when required, served in the king's longships for the defence of the island. Each of the island's six 'skeid-things' provided crews for four ships, thereby providing the king with sufficient crews for 24 warships.

The entrance to Sulby Glen is at the
Tholt-e-Will Hotel, and in 1894
admission was only a few pence. The
glen features two waterfalls, the Alt and
the Tholt-e-Will, of which the former is
the more impressive.

SULBY
Tholt-e-Will Bridge 1894
A favourite outing with holidaymakers
was to take the Snaefell Mountain
Railway to where it crossed the Douglas
to Ramsey road at the Bungalow Hotel,
and then walk along the road through
the valley to the Tholt-e-Will Hotel and
Sulby Glen.

SULBY, THE WATERFALL 1894 34661

SULBY, THOLT-E-WILL BRIDGE 1894 34660

SULBY GLEN 1894 34659
Lying between Mount Karrin and Slieav Managh, Sulby Glen was often referred to by the Victorians as 'the Manx Switzerland', though the compilers of the Baedecker Guides thought the place more reminiscent of the Scottish Highlands.

SULBY, THE FOOTBRIDGE AND PRIMROSE HILL 1894 34655
The Manx Electric Railway was quick to capitalise on the popularity of Sulby Glen by offering personally conducted tours. For an all-in price, tourists travelled from Derby Castle to Laxey, where they boarded a Snaefell Mountain Railway car to the Bungalow. From the Bungalow they were taken by charabanc to Sulby Glen, where they were free to explore the area before making the return journey. The price included lunch at the Tholt-e-Will Hotel and admission to the glen.

SULBY, THE BRIDGE 1894 34654

Sulby not only gives its name to the island's longest river but also to (probably) its tallest inhabitant. Arthur Caley, the eleventh of twelve children and known as the Sulby Giant, was 7 ft 6 ins tall, and weighed in at 44 stone. Arthur's height landed him a job with Barnum & Bailey's circus.

GLEN AULDYN 1894 34650

Today what is now the B16 road runs from Milntown to Glen Auldyn and the Brookdale Plantation. In Victorian and Edwardian times there was a popular walk from Tholt-e-Will to Ramsey by way of Glen Auldyn.

GLEN AULDYN
General View 1894
This beautiful glen is situated to the
north east of Snaefell with steep slopes
on either side.

◆

GLEN AULDYN
A Hideaway 1894
The 1906 Baedecker Guide states that
'in July and August especially, Douglas
and its neighbourhood are practically
the playground for the operatives of
Lancashire and Yorkshire, but at other
seasons and in the smaller town and
country districts the 'tripper' element is
not conspicuous'. It looks as though our
man is on his own.

GLEN AULDYN, GENERAL VIEW 1894 34653

GLEN AULDYN, A HIDEAWAY 1894 34651

RAMSEY, THE TOWN 1895 36739
Situated on the north-east coast, Ramsey in
the 1890s was a small town of around 4,500
people. For the visitor, hotel accommodation
was cheaper than at Douglas; rooms at the
Queen's, Prince of Wales, and Albion started
from 2s 6d per day. Full board at the Imperial
would set you back 6s-7s a day.

RAMSEY, ON THE SANDS 1895 36744
Though the shore to the south of Ramsey is rocky, a stroll along it at low tide was a popular Victorian way of taking some gentle exercise. Following a visit by Edward VII in 1902, the town styled itself 'Royal Ramsey', and why not? After all, Queen Victoria and Prince Albert had also visited the town back in 1847.

RAMSEY, THE PARK 1895 36741
The Mooragh Park, Lake, and Golf Links were part of a major development begun in 1887 that also included Mooragh Promenade with its fine late-Victorian terraced properties. For those of you who know Mooragh Promenade, the gaps between the terraces are not due to demolition; the houses were never built.

RAMSEY, THE SOUTH PROMENADE 1894 33059
At the height of the season the South Promenade would often be crowded with holidaymakers. The more energetic and adventurous could make their way to the small wooden shed with the sloping roof, where they could hire cycles by the day, week, or longer. This area of the town was redeveloped in the 1970s with the building of the multi-storey Queen's and King's Courts.

MAUGHOLD, THE VILLAGE 1895 36733

Maughold is one of a number of places on the island named after Celtic saints. The legend of Maughold is that he was a pirate or brigand, who, seeing the error of his ways, allowed himself to be cast adrift in a leather boat, his arms and legs shackled. The boat drifted ashore on Man and Maughold told his story to the local bishop. He became a hermit and the fame of his piety spread. It was Maughold who gave the veil of virginity to St Bridget when she visited him in AD 498.

MAUGHOLD, THE CHURCH AND CROSS 1895   36735

MAUGHOLD, THE CROSS 1895   36736

MAUGHOLD
The Church and Cross 1895

On the 14th-century pillared cross is one of the earliest surviving representations of the Three Legs of Man. The other is on the Manx Sword of State which Olaf Godreson is said to have owned c1230. The device was used as early as 1310 by Henry de Bello Morte, Lord of Man. It might derive from a triple knot design used by the Norse-Irish kings of Dublin, or from the swastika.

◆

MAUGHOLD
The Cross 1895

As well as the cross there are three examples of keeills at Maughold, one of which can be seen here. These are early Christian single-chambered chapels, nearly 200 of which are known to have existed. They were constructed with daub and wattle or stone walls with thatched roofs. Some had a window and/or an altar at the eastern end; the door was at the western end.

DHOON GLEN 1894 34646

DHOON GLEN 1894
In Manx, 'Dhoon' means fort, though
this structure is the nearest to a
fortification. As with other glens, Dhoon
also had its hotel, a wooden affair at the
entrance which burnt down in 1932 and
was never rebuilt.

DHOON GLEN
The Waterfall 1894
Dhoon Glen is now a Manx National
Heritage site of special ecological
importance, as there are plants here
which are not found anywhere else on
the island, and others that are rare in
Man. It is also a site of
geological interest.

DHOON GLEN, THE WATERFALL 1894 34644

LAXEY, THE HARBOUR 1894 34639
The Laxey mines had one distinct
advantage over those at Foxdale - they
had a nearby harbour from which ore
could be exported direct. Perhaps it was
this small advantage that enabled the
Laxey mines to survive a few years longer
than those at Foxdale. Other reasons
why the mining industry failed were
foreign competition and
geological exhaustion.

LAXEY
The Waterfall 1896
This photographs shows the waterfall, and above that the T-rocker viaduct of the Lady Isabella. In 1930 a flash flood swept down Laxey Valley with sufficient force to destroy the central section of the T-rocker, though it was later restored.

◆

LAXEY
The Wheel 1896
Designed by Manxman Robert Casement and commissioned in September 1854 to pump water from the Laxey mines, the wheel was in regular use until 1920. It is named Lady Isabella in honour of Lady Isabella Hope, wife of Governor Hope. When this picture was taken, the mining company charged visitors 3d each to use the observation platform. In 1854, Laxey Mining's £80 paid shares were trading at £1,200 each.

LAXEY, THE WATERFALL 1896 37208

LAXEY, THE WHEEL 1896 37206

LAXEY, GENERAL VIEW 1894 34641

A number of cottages in Laxey were built by George William Dumbell, chairman of the Laxey Mining Co, for his miners and their families. He also donated land for a chapel. Dumbell's Row still stands, as do other links with Laxey's mining past; the Station Hotel was once the Mine Captain's house.

LAXEY, VIEW OF THE GARDENS 1894 34643

Laxey's popularity with holidaymakers grew after the opening of the coast electric tramway. The operators of Laxey Glen Gardens were among the pioneers of today's leisure and theme parks. Visitors paid an entrance fee, the entertainments were free: tennis, quoits, bowling, croquet, hobby horses, swings, and brass band concerts.

CAPTAIN'S HOUSE. LAXEY, FROM THE WHEEL LOOKING EAST 1894 34640
Looking towards Laxey Harbour with Laxey Head to the left and South Cape to the right. Apart from mining, Laxey was also home to Corlett's flour mill, built in 1860 by the then Captain of the Laxey mines. It supplied a booming local market and was capable of competing against mainland mills.

SNAEFELL, SUMMIT STATION 1897 39890

The Snaefell Mountain Railway opened for traffic in August 1895. It operates on the Fell system, whereby a third rail is laid in the centre of the track. This is gripped by wheels that ensure the car stays on the rails, and by brake shoes that provide additional braking on the line's severe gradients. In 1897 a return trip up Snaefell from Laxey cost 2s return.

SNAEFELL, THE SUMMIT 1897 39888

On sunny days, Snaefell summit (2034 ft) offers the visitor superb views of England, Ireland and Scotland. In 1906 the Summit Hotel was rebuilt in the castellated style complete with turrets. Unfortunately, it was badly damaged by fire in 1982 and restoration work has left a much plainer building.

GARWICK, THE BEACH AND GLEN 1896 37203
Situated between Groudle Glen and Laxey, Garwick was just twenty minutes away from Douglas on the Manx
Electric Tramway, but it looks as though our intrepid cameraman had the place all to himself. The view is
towards Laxey Bay and Gob y Rheynn.

GARWICK, THE HOTEL 1896 37205
There were hotels at or near most of the glens. Prices for a pension (room, meals and service) at the glen hotels
were on a par with those charged by some of the Peel and Port St Mary hotels for similar arrangements.

GROUDLE GLEN 1894 34635

GROUDLE GLEN, LHEN COAN 1894 34637

GROUDLE GLEN 1894
The vast majority of day visitors to the island rarely strayed beyond Douglas and Onchan, but the opening of the first section of the Manx Electric Railway in September 1893 brought Groudle Glen within easy reach. Situated just two and a half miles from Douglas, the Glen is known as 'the Fern Land of Mona'.

◆

GROUDLE GLEN
Lhen Coan 1894
In 1896 Groudle Glen opened its own railway from Lhen Coan station to a terminus at Sea Lion Cove, and at less than one mile in length it was one of the shortest passenger-carrying railways in the world. Not only were the passengers treated to some wonderful natural scenery, there were also enclosures for both polar bears and sea lions. Lhen Coan translates as 'lovely Glen'.

GROUDLE GLEN
The Waterwheel 1907
The Groudle Glen waterwheel is somewhat smaller than the Lady Isabella. It was built neither to grind corn, drive machinery, nor pump out a mine. It was of no practical use, having been built purely as an attraction for Edwardian visitors.

◆

GROUDLE GLEN
The Rustic Path 1894
Only a year earlier Mr R M Broadbent had opened the Groudle Glen Hotel as part of a continuing series of improvements to attract visitors. The natural beauty of the glen could be experienced by taking the rustic walkways to the rocky and often breezy headland with its deep inlets.

GROUDLE GLEN, THE WATERWHEEL 1907 59178

GROUDLE GLEN, THE RUSTIC PATH 1894 34636

PORT SODERICK, THE BEACH 1893 33026
Port Soderick was developed in the 1890s by the Forrester family, and was one of the first attractions created for the tourist industry. It was close enough to Douglas to entice day trippers to pay a visit.

PORT SODERICK, THE HOTEL 1893 33028
On the left of the picture is a poster advertising a sacred concert at the Bijou Theatre, one of a number of ways in which Victorian holidaymakers could celebrate their Christian faith. During the season, open-air services were held at Douglas Head, and of course there were the tremendously popular services at Kirk Bradden, some of which are said to have attracted congregations approaching 20,000 people.

PORT SODERICK
The Caves 1893

An 1896 official guide states that Port Soderick is the most popular pleasure resort on Man, 'Romantic, Natural and the only FREE Glen on the island'. Even the smugglers' caves are free.

◆

PORT SODERICK
The Hotel 1903

A few improvements have been made in the ten years since the previous pictures of Port Soderick were taken. The hotel has acquired a canopied front, and the inclined tramway (formally located at the Falcon Cliff Hotel, Douglas) has been rebuilt here to link the resort with the terminus of the Douglas Southern Electric Tramway. For a fare of 6d each way, the DSET offered passengers an exciting cliff-edge ride between Port Soderick and Douglas Head.

PORT SODERICK, THE CAVES 1893 33029

PORT SODERICK, THE HOTEL 1903 50662

PORT SODERICK, THE BEACH 1907 59174
The Forrester family even had their own
steamer, the 'Katrina', which used to ply
between Port Soderick and Douglas, but it was
the IOMR who played a major part in
promoting the resort by operating special
excursion trains. Business was so good that in
1896 the IOMR rebuilt the station.

DERBY HAVEN. FORT ISLAND 1897 39897

The southern end of Derby Haven is protected by St Michael's Island with its ruined chapel, Derby fort and battery. In this view the Frith cameraman has included part of the broad sweep of Castletown Bay. St Michael's Island is now a Manx Heritage site.

DERBY HAVEN, THE GOLF LINKS HOTEL 1903 50672

In the ten years or so prior to the Great War, golf went through a boom with a large number of courses opening throughout the UK. Professionals like James Braid were often engaged to give an exhibition match on the opening day. One such course hired a full military band - try timing shots to the strains of 'Annie Laurie' - but Braid got his own back on the last green when he put his ball straight through the big bass drum.

DERBYHAVEN 1897 39898

In 1823 John Butcher, a preacher from Bolton, was landed by fishing boat at Derbyhaven and brought Primitive Methodism to the island. The movement's birthplace was at Mow Cop, Staffordshire, where Hugh Bourne and William Clowes held their first meetings in 1807. They were later expelled from the Methodist Conference and took the name Primitive Methodists in 1811.

DERBYHAVEN, THE DERBY HAVEN HOTEL 1903 50671

Visitors to the Castletown area had a choice of hotels; the Castletown Hotel, the Derby Haven, the Marine Hydro Hotel (where hydropathic treatments could be taken), and the Golf Links Hotel which offered a pension (room, meals, service) for 6s 6d per day.

DERBY HAVEN, LOOKING TOWARDS CASTLETOWN 1897 39896
If coal was burned in these houses, it had to be imported
from the mainland. There have been a number of attempts
to find coal on Man, with much of the exploration work
concentrated on the northern part of the island. In 1985-86
Rio Tinto Zinc carried out borings near Peel,
Derbyhaven and Ballasalla.

CASTLETOWN, KING WILLIAM'S COLLEGE 1897 39895
The distinctive central tower of King William's College was designed by John Welch and was a feature of a major rebuilding programme following a fire in 1844. This picture was taken the year one of the college's famous old boys, Thomas E Brown, died. Born in 1830, the year the college opened, Brown was a poet, scholar, and Fellow of Oriel College.

CASTLETOWN, FROM THE PIER 1893 33025
This view looks towards King William's College, Derbyhaven and St Michael's Island. Near the college is Hango Hill, the scene in 1663 of the execution of the Manx patriot William Christian (Illian Dohne) for his role in the rebellion of 1651. He was sentenced to be hanged, drawn and quartered but this was commuted to shooting by a firing squad on account of his wife's 'inconsolable condition'. He was shot before news of his successful appeal to Charles II reached Man.

CASTLETOWN, FROM THE PIER 1893 33024

The rocky entrance to Castletown meant that the harbour remained under-developed and under-used for years. In 1955 Douglas handled around 70 per cent of the island's imports and exports, while Castletown accounted for less than 4 per cent of imports and no exports. Things improved in the mid-1970s when Castletown was upgraded to handle a container service, resulting in the port handling 15 per cent of imports and 20 per cent of exports.

CASTLETOWN, FROM THE PIER 1903 50650

Little has changed since picture No 33024 was taken, save for the building of a lifeboat station. St Mary's was rebuilt in the 1830s, replacing the church built by Bishop Thomas Wilson in 1701. Wilson was appointed Bishop of Sodor and Man in 1698, having previously served as chaplain to the ninth Earl of Derby.

CASTLETOWN, CASTLE RUSHEN 1903 50656

The present Castle Rushen dates from the 12th to the 14th centuries. It was here in 1265 that Magnus, last of Man's Norse kings, died. With his death began nearly seventy years of Scottish rule until the island was taken by Edward III of England. The Doric column was erected as a memorial to Colonel Cornelious Smelt who was Lieutenant-Governor of the island between 1805-32.

CASTLETOWN, CASTLE RUSHEN 1903 50658

When William Montacute, Earl of Salisbury, was appointed First Lord of Man he chose Castletown for his capital. Montacute strengthened the fortress defences, adding a new tower on the eastern side and a twin-towered gateway. Later 14th-century improvements included a curtain wall and the heightening of the keep. The glacis was added by Cardinal Wolsey in c1540 while he was serving as a trustee for the underage Earl of Derby.

CASTLETOWN
Castle Rushen c1885

In the early 1720s Bishop Wilson was held prisoner in Castle Rushen for nine weeks for failing to pay a fine. In 1722 an ecclesiastical court found a certain Lady Horne guilty of slander. Lady Horne happened to be the wife of the Governor, who was none too pleased.

The Governor declared that ecclesiastical courts were acting illegally and that they must drop all such cases. The Bishop and his vicars-general refused and finished up in jail themselves.

◆

CASTLETOWN
Castle Rushen 1893

In 1312 England was on the brink of civil war. Robert the Bruce seized the advantage by dispatching his brother Edward, together with James Douglas, into northern England. They sacked a number of towns, including Durham and Hartlepool, while Robert reduced England's Scottish possessions to a handful of fortresses. In 1313 Robert invaded Man, besieging and almost destroying Castle Rushen in the process.

CASTLETOWN, CASTLE RUSHEN c1885 C47501

CASTLETOWN, CASTLE RUSHEN 1893 33021

CASTLETOWN, THE STACK 1903 50653

Castletown lies within the island's carboniferous limestone area. The west side of the bay comprises Scarlett Point, which has outcrops of lava and volcanic ash, while the stack is columnar basalt. The east side of the bay features the flat rocks of Langness Point.

COLBY, THE VILLAGE 1897 39899

The small farming community of Colby is thought to have derived its name from Colli's farm, 'by' being a Scandinavian word for a farm or homestead. The village at this time is an unspoilt mix of traditional single-storey thatched crofts and solid-looking two-storey stone houses.

COLBY, THE VILLAGE 1897 39900

The Frith cameraman had only a few ducks for company when he took this picture in 1897, one of a series for possible use within the Frith postcard range. Postcards could be sent at half the letter rate, but in those days nothing could be written on them apart from the recipient's address. It was only after 1902 that a message could also be added.

COLBY, THE GLEN 1897 39901

The opening of the IOM Railway meant that Colby Glen was within easy reach of holidaymakers based in Douglas. By rail Castletown was only seven minutes away, Port Erin eight minutes, and Port St Mary seven minutes.

COLBY
The Waterfall 1897
This waterfall is not as spectacular as the Rhenass falls of Glen Helen or those of Glen Meay or Dhoon Glen, but even so the Frith cameraman managed to provide us with a pleasing view of the Colby falls.

◆

PORT ST MARY
Street and Harbour 1895
In Manx folklore the village was named 'the Harbour of Mary' in honour of the Blessed Virgin by Celtic missionaries, who founded a chapel here. Missionaries from Ireland began arriving in the 5th century; it is possible that St Patrick himself founded the church on St Patrick's Isle, Peel.

COLBY, THE WATERFALL 1897 39902

PORT ST MARY, STREET AND HARBOUR 1895 39908

PORT ST MARY, THE HARBOUR 1903 50645

It was to Port St Mary that the Scottish granite to be used in the construction of Chicken Rock Lighthouse was brought, and where each stone was cut and dressed to size before being taken out to the site. The lighthouse was built in the mid-1870s.

Port St Mary, The Harbour 1895 35935
The old pier was opened in 1845 having cost
£8,200 to construct. It was 615 feet long, and
provided the village with good anchorage
facilities for small craft and fishing vessels.
However, with the opening of the £39,000
Alfred Pier in 1882, Port St Mary was able to
offer deep-water berthing.

PORT ST MARY, GENERAL VIEW 1895 35946
By the 1890s, Port St Mary was rapidly establishing a
reputation as a resort for the genteel classes. Hotel
and residential developments were soon under way,
and in 1898 the Isle of Man Railway completely rebuilt
the station and added a new hotel. Among the hotels
that visitors could choose from in 1906 were the Cliff
Hotel (rooms 2s, dinner from 2s 6d), or the Shore,
where full board cost from 5s 6d per day.

PORT ST MARY, THE BEACH 1895 35944
At this time Port St Mary was still being described
as a 'pleasant little fishing port and seaside resort'.
The local fishing fleet was, however, in decline. By
the late 1890s the local fleet comprised 56 boats
employing 346 men and boys, landing an annual
catch valued at less than £3,000.

CREGNEISH, THE VILLAGE 1897 39903

Cregneish lies between Port St Mary and the Calf of Man. When this picture was taken, most of the villagers would have earned their living from agriculture or fishing, or both. A number of properties, including a weaver's cottage and a farmstead, now comprise the National Folk Museum, and are fitted out to portray village life as it was around 1900.

CREGNEISH, MEAYLL CIRCLE 1897 39904

There are a number of Neolithic monuments on the island; the Meayll Circle is of a unique design with six pairs of lintel graves arranged in a circle. When the site was excavated in 1893, evidence of burnt human bones were unearthed, along with Neolithic pottery. Other important sites include Cashtal-Yn-Ard and the chambered cairn near Laxey known as King Orrey's Grave.

SPANISH HEAD
Sugar Loaf Rock 1895

The cliffs in this part of the island are important breeding grounds for sea birds. Other sites include the whole of Langness (which is designated a bird sanctuary), and the Ayres conservation area in the north of the island. Ayres is a unique heathland that supports diverse plant life and colonies of birds including oystercatchers, mallards, lapwings, arctic, common and little terns, and curlews.

CALF OF MAN 1897

In early 20th century guides, walkers were advised to leave the train at Port St Mary and go by way of the Chasms and Spanish Head to Port Erin.. The Chasms were described as fissures resembling those between Lydstep Cove and Manorbier Bay in Wales, and caused by the falling in of caves. At Spanish Head they would be offered a commanding view of the Calf of Man.

SPANISH HEAD, SUGAR LOAF ROCK 1895   36762

CALF OF MAN 1897   39913

CALF OF MAN, FROM BRADDA HEAD 1895 35932

The Calf of Man looking in the general direction of Kione Beg and Gibdale Point. The narrow channel which separates the island from Man, Calf Sound, is over on the left of the picture. There was a lighthouse on the Calf until 1875, when it was closed in favour of a new one that had been constructed on the Chicken Rocks.

PORT ERIN, RUSHEN CHURCH 1907 59197

Here we see Kirk Rushen (Holy Trinity) with its bell turret and the vicarage. In more recent times the vicarage has lost its chimney stacks and ivy cladding, and the tree has been felled. The church now sports a large lych-gate.

PORT ERIN, ATHOL PARK 1907 59184

This is a late-Victorian development just off the seafront; the castellated roof of the Falcon's Nest Hotel can be seen rising above the terrace. It appears that there is plenty of landscaping work still to be done, and although one street lamp is in place, it is doubtful that it will give enough light for the whole terrace.

PORT ERIN, THE PROMENADE 1903 50629

This photograph gives us a good view of some of the late-Victorian seafront developments at Port Erin. The resort's popularity increased so much in the ten years or so prior to the outbreak of the Great War that the IOMR added a spacious platform during the 1904 rebuilding of the station. As passenger traffic continued to grow, the platform was extended again in 1911.

PORT ERIN, STATION ROAD 1907 59183
Built by McArd & Moore of best Ruabon red
brick, the IOMR station is on the right of the
picture. The windows on the platform side of
the nearer gable end are just visible, and are
designed in a style sometimes referred to as
'Mill-engine Gothic', as they are similar to
those often used to adorn the engine houses
of Lancashire mills.

PORT ERIN, THE BEACH 1897 39921
A bathing machine attracts a small crowd of
onlookers as it is dragged into the water by a
horse. The driver would stop when he
considered the water deep enough to allow
ladies to enter the sea in a manner in which
their modesty would be protected.

PORT ERIN, FROM THE CLIFF 1901 47239

The cottages and buildings along the beach belong to the earliest settlement, while the later Victorian developments are strung out along the higher ground. Port Erin's increasing popularity with holidaymakers led to a number of hotels being opened, including the Falcon's Nest, the Eagle, the Bellevue, and the Bay.

PORT ERIN, THE BEACH 1897 39922

In 1842 Port Erin was chosen as the location for a Marine Biological Station; it still exists, though these days it is a part of the University of Liverpool. One of the great pioneers in marine biology, Professor Edward Forbes, was born at Douglas in 1815. Before his untimely death in 1854 he was already the President of the Geological Society. The station can be seen here on the right on the far side of the bay.

PORT ERIN, THE HARBOUR 1897 39925

Whether it be Blackpool, Dunoon, Port Bannatyne, Port Erin or any of a hundred other resorts in the 1890s, holidaymakers had developed a passion for messing about in boats, mainly of the rowing variety, though there were also adventurous souls prepared to hire out yachts. With clear skies and a calm sea, it looks as though the local boatmen are in for a profitable day.

PORT ERIN, THE BATHS 1907 59195

Mixed bathing - whatever next! They'll be wanting to give women the vote! But on the enlightened Isle of Man they already had it. Women were given the vote in 1881; the first woman member of the House of Keys was Mrs Marion Shimmin, elected in February 1933.

PORT ERIN, THE BAY 1901 47241

PORT ERIN
The Bay 1901
The decline of the herring fishery was offset to a certain extent by dredging for scallops and queenies. In 1937 the first dredging operations on a commercial scale were undertaken around Port Erin. It is estimated that 65 per cent of the scallop population in the Irish Sea is to be found within Manx waters. By the 1980s, half of all scallops caught in the Irish Sea were being landed in Man.

◆

PORT ERIN
From the Breakwater 1894
Port Erin breakwater had a short life. Work began in 1864, but in 1868, while still under construction, it was badly damaged by a storm; it was not until the following year that Tynwald voted funds for repairs and completion.

PORT ERIN, FROM THE BREAKWATER 1894 34665

PORT ERIN, GENERAL VIEW 1895 35923
As well as the development along the seafront, we can see the awnings on the shops along Station Road, the station, and the terrace known as Athol Park. In the distance is the valley leading to Fleshwick Bay.

PORT ERIN, DISTANT VIEW 1897 39914
In this view we can clearly see the old fishing village at the water's edge and the later developments associated with the resort of Port Erin. In the distance to the left are Bradda Hill, Bradda West and Bradda East.

PORT ERIN, BRADDA 1907 59190
By the time this picture was taken, Port Erin
had been transformed from a fishing village
into a popular resort. Development spread
beyond the immediate area of the town to
Bradda West and Bradda East; many of the
houses in this picture have been built since
picture No 47241 was taken in 1901.

PORT ERIN, FROM BRADDA HEAD 1895 35931

PORT ERIN
From Bradda Head 1895
This view looks towards Bay Fine, Aldrick and the Calf of Man. We can also see the remains of the breakwater, which by 1870 had become the subject of a wrangle between Tynwald and the Imperial Government that was not resolved until 1879. Damaged again in 1882, and repaired in 1883, the breakwater was finally destroyed by yet another storm in 1884.

◆

PORT ERIN
The Hut 1907
This charming hut has a thatched roof, leaded windows and ivy-clad walls. There is greenery inside the porch, and the old man sitting in the doorway completes the picturesque ensemble by sporting a long beard.

PORT ERIN, THE HUT 1907 59193

PORT ERIN, BRADDA HEAD 1895 35930

PORT ERIN
Bradda Head 1895

Some of the earliest mining on the island was carried out at Bradda Head. In 1246 King Harald Olaveson granted mining rights to the monks of both Furness Abbey and Rushen Abbey, though written records of their activities have still to be discovered.

◆

PORT ERIN
Milner Tower 1901

The tower was erected on Bradda Head in 1871 to the memory of William Milner, a Liverpool safe manufacturer who did much to ease the lot of local fishermen and their families.

PORT ERIN, MILNER TOWER 1901 47244

PORT ERIN, SUNSET AT BRADDA HEAD 1897 39927
As the sun goes down, the only activity at sea
comes from fishing boats and one
or two yachtsmen.

PORT ERIN, SUNSET OFF BRADDA HEAD 1903 50636
The mine was at the foot of the cliff, and in 1656 Captain Edward Christian found Bradda contained 'lead ore with much silver'. In 1699 the mine's output was 164 tonnes.

FLESHWICK BAY 1895 35933
Nestling between Bradda and the lower slopes of Cronk-ny-Irree-Laa, Fleshwick Bay is less than two miles north of Port Erin and reached by way of Ballaglonney. In 1895, Fleshwick presented visitors to Port Erin with an opportunity enjoy a little seclusion away from the main resort area.

FLESHWICK BAY 1897 39928
The coastline of the Isle of Man is one of outstanding natural beauty. There is the Sugar Loaf Rock at Spanish Head, the caves at Port Soderick, and in the north east the Maughold Brooghs - a Manx Heritage site that stretches from Port e Vullen to Grob ny Strona. Here at Fleshwick, visitors can explore this superb natural arch.

Index

Frith Book Co 1999 Titles

From 2000 we aim at publishing 100 new books each year. For latest catalogue please contact Frith Book Co

Barnstaple	1-85937-084-5	£12.99	Oct 99
Blackpool	1-85937-049-7	£12.99	Oct 99
Bognor Regis	1-85937-055-1	£12.99	Oct 99
Bristol	1-85937-050-0	£12.99	Oct 99
Cambridge	1-85937-092-6	£12.99	Nov 99
Cambridgeshire	1-85937-086-1	£14.99	Nov 99
Cheshire	1-85937-045-4	£14.99	Oct 99
Chester	1-85937-090-X	£12.99	Nov 99
Chesterfield	1-85937-071-3	£12.99	Oct 99
Chichester	1-85937-089-6	£12.99	Nov 99
Cornwall	1-85937-054-3	£14.99	Oct 99
Cotswolds	1-85937-099-3	£14.99	Nov 99

Maidstone	1-85937-056-X	£12.99	Oct 99
Northumberland & Tyne and Wear	1-85937-072-1	£14.99	Sep 99
North Yorkshire	1-85937-048-9	£14.99	Oct 99
Nottingham	1-85937-060-8	£12.99	Oct 99
Oxfordshire	1-85937-076-4	£14.99	Oct 99
Penzance	1-85937-069-1	£12.99	Oct 99
Reading	1-85937-087-X	£12.99	Nov 99
St Ives	1-85937-068-3	£12.99	Oct 99
Salisbury	1-85937-091-8	£12.99	Nov 99
Scarborough	1-85937-104-3	£12.99	Oct 99
Scottish Castles	1-85937-077-2	£14.99	Nov 99
Sevenoaks and Tonbridge	1-85937-057-8	£12.99	Oct 99
Sheffield and S Yorkshire	1-85937-070-5	£12.99	Oct 99
Shropshire	1-85937-083-7	£14.99	Nov 99
Southampton	1-85937-088-8	£12.99	Nov 99
Staffordshire	1-85937-047-0	£14.99	Nov 99
Stratford upon Avon	1-85937-098-5	£12.99	Nov 99
Suffolk	1-85937-074-8	£14.99	Nov 99
Surrey	1-85937-081-0	£14.99	Nov 99
Torbay	1-85937-063-2	£12.99	Oct 99
Wiltshire	1-85937-053-5	£14.99	Oct 99

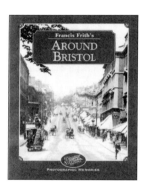
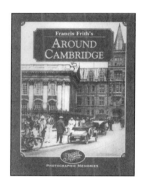

Derby	1-85937-046-2	£12.99	Oct 99
Devon	1-85937-052-7	£14.99	Oct 99
Dorset	1-85937-075-6	£14.99	Oct 99
Dorset Coast	1-85937-062-4	£14.99	Nov 99
Dublin	1-85937-058-6	£12.99	Oct 99
East Anglia	1-85937-059-4	£14.99	Oct 99
Eastbourne	1-85937-061-6	£12.99	Oct 99
English Castles	1-85937-078-0	£14.99	Oct 99
Essex	1-85937-082-9	£14.99	Nov 99
Falmouth	1-85937-066-7	£12.99	Oct 99
Hampshire	1-85937-064-0	£14.99	Nov 99
Hertfordshire	1-85937-079-9	£14.99	Nov 99
Isle of Man	1-85937-065-9	£14.99	Nov 99
Liverpool	1-85937-051-9	£12.99	Sep 99

British Life A Century Ago

246 x 189mm 144pp, hardback. Black and white Lavishly illustrated with photos from the turn of the century, and with extensive commentary. It offers a unique insight into the social history and heritage of bygone Britain.

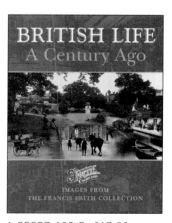

1-85937-103-5 £17.99

Available from your local bookshop or from the publisher

FRITH PRODUCTS & SERVICES

Francis Frith would doubtless be pleased to know that the pioneering publishing venture he started in 1860 still continues today. More than a hundred and thirty years later, The Francis Frith Collection continues in the same innovative tradition and is now one of the foremost publishers of vintage photographs in the world. Some of the current activities include:

Interior Decoration

Today Frith's photographs can be seen framed and as giant wall murals in thousands of pubs, restaurants, hotels, banks, retail stores and other public buildings throughout the country. In every case they enhance the unique local atmosphere of the places they depict and provide reminders of gentler days in an increasingly busy and frenetic world.

Product Promotions

Frith products have been used by many major companies to promote the sales of their own products or to reinforce their own history and heritage. Brands include Hovis bread, Courage beers, Scots Porage Oats, Colman's mustard, Cadbury's foods, Mellow Birds coffee, Dunhill pipe tobacco, Guinness, and Bulmer's Cider.

Genealogy and Family History

As the interest in family history and roots grows world-wide, more and more people are turning to Frith's photographs of Great Britain for images of the towns, villages and streets where their ancestors lived; and, of course, photographs of the churches and chapels where their ancestors were christened, married and buried are an essential part of every genealogy tree and family album.

A series of easy-to-use CD Roms is planned for publication, and an increasing number of Frith photographs will be able to be viewed on specialist genealogy sites. A growing range of Frith books will be available on CD.

The Internet

Already thousands of Frith photographs can be viewed and purchased on the internet. By the end of the year 2000 some 60,000 Frith photographs will be available on the internet. The number of sites is constantly expanding, each focussing on different products and services from the Collection.

Some of the sites are listed below.

www.townpages.co.uk
www.familystorehouse.com
www.britannia.com
www.icollector.com
www.barclaysquare.co.uk
www.cornwall-online.co.uk

For background information on the Collection look at the two following sites:

www.francisfrith.com
www.francisfrith.co.uk

Frith Products

All Frith photographs are available Framed or just as Mounted Prints, and can be ordered from the address below. From time to time other products - Address Books, Calendars, Table Mats, Postcards etc - are available.

The Frith Collectors' Guild

In response to the many customers who enjoy collecting Frith photographs we have created the Frith Collectors' Guild. Members are entitled to a range of benefits, including a regular magazine, special discounts and special limited edition products.

For further information: if you would like further information on any of the above aspects of the Frith business please contact us at the address below:

The Francis Frith Collection, Frith's Barn, Teffont, Salisbury, Wiltshire England SP3 5QP.
Tel: +44 (0) 1722 716 376 Fax: +44 (0) 1722 716 881   Email: frithbook.co.uk

To receive your FREE Mounted Print

Cut out this Voucher and return it with your remittance for £1.50 to cover postage and handling. Choose any photograph included in this book. Your SEPIA print will be A4 in size, and mounted in a cream mount with burgundy rule lines, overall size 14 x 11 inches.

Order additional Mounted Prints at HALF PRICE (only £7.49 each*)

If there are further pictures you would like to order, possibly as gifts for friends and family, acquire them at half price (no additional postage and handling required).

Have your Mounted Prints framed*

For an additional £14.95 per print you can have your chosen Mounted Print framed in an elegant polished wood and gilt moulding, overall size 16 x 13 inches (no additional postage and handling required).

---

* IMPORTANT!
These special prices are only available if ordered using the original voucher on this page (no copies permitted) and at the same time as your free Mounted Print, for delivery to the same address

---

Voucher for FREE and Reduced Price Frith Prints

Picture no.	Page number	Qty	Mounted @ £7.49	Framed + £14.95	Total Cost
		1	**Free of charge***	£	£
			£	£	£
			£	£	£
			£	£	£
			£	£	£
			£	£	£
			* Post & handling		£1.50
			Total Order Cost		£

Title: ISLE OF MAN
065-9

Please do not photocopy this voucher. Only the original is valid, so please cut it out and return it to us.

I enclose a cheque / postal order for £ . . . .
made payable to 'The Francis Frith Collection'
OR please debit my Mastercard / Visa / Switch / Amex card

Number . . . .

Expires . . . . Signature . . . .

Name Mr/Mrs/Ms . . . .

Address . . . .

. . . .

. . . .

. . . .

. . . . Postcode . . . .

Daytime Tel No . . . . Valid to 31/12/01

Frith Collectors' Guild

From time to time we publish a magazine of news and stories about Frith photographs and further special offers of Frith products. If you would like 12 months FREE membership, please return this form and we will send you a New Member Pack.

Send completed forms to:
The Francis Frith Collection, Frith's Barn, Teffont, Salisbury, Wiltshire SP3 5QP

The Francis Frith Collectors' Guild

I would like to receive the New Members Pack offering 12 months FREE membership.
065-9

Name Mr/Mrs/Ms . . . .

Address . . . .

. . . .

. . . .

. . . . Postcode . . . .